# Viola Time Sprinters

## Piano accompaniment book

### Kathy and David Blackwell

**Teacher's note**

These piano parts are written to accompany the tunes in *Viola Time Sprinters*. They are an alternative to the viola duet accompaniments or CD, and are not designed to be used with those items.

Kathy and David Blackwell

MUSIC DEPARTMENT

OXFORD

UNIVERSITY PRESS

**OXFORD**
UNIVERSITY PRESS

Great Clarendon Street, Oxford OX2 6DP,
United Kingdom

Oxford University Press is a department of the University of Oxford.
It furthers the University's objective of excellence in research, scholarship,
and education by publishing worldwide. Oxford is a registered trade mark of
Oxford University Press in the UK and in certain other countries

ISBN 978-0-19-339852-8

Cover illustration by Martin Remphry

Music and text origination by Katie Johnston
Printed in Great Britain on acid-free paper by
Halstan & Co. Ltd, Amersham, Bucks.

# Contents

The unaccompanied rounds from the viola book are not included in this book.

# 1. Ready to rock

KB & DB

# 2. Clear skies

KB & DB

# 3. Ode to joy

## (from Symphony No. 9)

Ludwig van Beethoven (1770–1827)

# 4. Song from the show

KB & DB

# 5. Starry night

KB & DB

# 6. Paris café

KB & DB

# 8. Jacob's dance

KB & DB

Nos. 7 and 8 are reversed to avoid a page turn.

# 7. Gaudete!

Medieval carol

# 9. Sprint finish

KB & DB

The viola part is written out in full.

# 10. Bolero

Spanish trad.

This piece can be played as a solo or duet with piano, or as an unaccompanied viola duet.
The viola parts are written out in full.

# 11. William Tell

G. A. Rossini (1792–1868)

# 12. Country gardens

English Morris Dance tune

# 13. You and me

KB & DB

# 14. The road to Donegal

KB & DB

# 15. *Full circle*

KB & DB

# 16. Thirsty work

KB & DB

Return to the chorus after each verse. The music is written out in full in the viola part.
The chorus and verse 1 can be played in semiquavers with spiccato bowing, as demonstrated in the final chorus on the CD.

# 17. Farewell to Skye

KB & DB

# 18. Lady Katherine's pavane

KB & DB

The pavane was a slow, stately court dance popular in the 16th and 17th centuries.

# 19. Dance of the Sugar Plum Fairy

(from the *Nutcracker* ballet)

P. I. Tchaikovsky (1840–93)

# 20. Allegro in D

G. P. Telemann (1681–1767)

Try starting this piece with either a down or an up bow.

## 22. Mexican fiesta

KB & DB

Nos. 21 and 22 are reversed to avoid a page turn.

# 21. Still reeling

(based on *Blair Atholl*, trad. Scottish reel)

arr. KB & DB

Add your own dynamics to this reel.

Verse 2

*Reel* **D.C.**

Verse 3

*Reel* **D.C.**

# 23. Show stopper

KB & DB

# 24. Spy movie

KB & DB

# 26. Hornpipe

(from the *Water Music*)

G. F. Handel (1685–1759)

Nos. 25 and 26 are reversed to avoid a page turn.

# 25. Largo

### (from the *New World* Symphony)

Antonín Dvořák (1841–1904)

# 27. Hungarian folk dance

KB & DB

# 28. Wild West

KB & DB

**Hoe-down**

# 29. Midnight song

KB & DB

# 30. Wade in the water

Spiritual

# 31. Dominant gene

KB & DB

# 32. Chromatic cats

KB & DB

# 33. Show off!

KB & DB

# 34. Little lamb

**Light and graceful**

Spiritual

The viola part is written out in full.

# 35. Habanera

### (from *Carmen*)

Georges Bizet (1838–75)

**Allegretto quasi Andantino**